"Harry the Mule is a delightful book that pairs knowledge of movement with lighthearted stories. The book is perfect for someone who wants to gain insight on injury prevention and pain management…I also learned that storytelling is an effective modality to help clients change for the better."
—Fern Cleary, OTR, Home Health Rehabilitation Supervisor

"I enjoyed the collection of sage advice mixed with stories of human 'mis-steps',…several of which I could identify with, and, I might add, learn from."
—Lilian C. Begg, former client,
World War 2 London Bombing 'Thriver'

"Now I'm convinced to listen to my body; my "Body awareness". Love the word-pictures in this book".
—Linda Barron, former client

"Karen knows how to make a story count, weaving it into a larger narrative…This is one of those books that will come back to mind because of the practical applications and the stories they are tucked into."
—Pastor Tim Tyler, Christian Counselor

"Humor really can be the best medicine. We can all take heed form the stories like Harry the Mule, to slow down and be more aware of ourselves. Karen does a marvelous job of intertwining humor with practical information that we can all benefit from."
—Jennifer Hines, RN, Home Health & Hospice nurse

"I enjoyed the book. Karen has a way of explaining 'down to earth' terms we can all understand and apply to our daily lives. As she worked with my husband, I was able to glean the information and principles she was teaching,…and use in my own activities"
—Roxzene Bockstruck, wife of former client

Harry the Mule ... and Other Injuries

Anecdotes and Antidotes to Life's Little Pains

Karen A. Shupp, PT, BSc. Biology

Harry the Mule … and Other Injuries
Anecdotes and Antidotes to Life's Little Pains

Copyright © 2021 by Karen A. Shupp, PT, BSc. Biology

Published by Bitterroot Mountain Publishing House LLC
4319 Echo Glenn Lane, Coeur d'Alene, ID 83815
BMPHmedia.com

Interior and cover design by Jera Publishing

All rights reserved. This book or parts thereof, may not be reproduced in any form without permission, except by a reviewer who may quote brief passages in a review to be printed in magazines, newspapers, or on the web.

The ideas, procedures, and suggestions in this book are intended to supplement, not replace, the medical and psychological advice of trained professionals. The author and publisher disclaim any liability arising directly or indirectly from the use of this book.

For permission to reproduce excerpts of this publication please contact: Bitterroot Mountain Publishing House at info@BMPHmedia.com

Library of Congress Control Number: 2021913849

ISBNs:
978-1-940025-51-3 (print)
978-1-940025-52-0 (eBook)

Printed in the United States of America

1.Injury 2. Wellness and physical therapy - book 3.Self-help healing 4.Pain-free - book 5.Physical therapy humor I. Title.

Dedication

This book is dedicated to my father, Charles Irwin Wright, DMD, who taught me about the love of life, healing and laughter. Thank you, Papa.

Acknowledgments

I wish to thank … well, everyone I have met in my life. Each person I have been in contact with, either on a personal level, or as a health practitioner, has provided me some form of important information; whether a pearl of wisdom to ease my life journey, or an "Aha!", an epiphany, as to why the Universe is as it is. Of course, not all these interactions were pleasant, but all provided insight into how I wished to live my life. Some of these moments appear within this book.

Highest gratitude to my publishing mentor and friend, E. Anna Goodwin, MS, NCC, for her insights and patience as I struggled through my first publishing experience. Much appreciation to my editor, Jennifer Leo and my professional co-workers who also provided valuable feedback.

I thank my husband, Darrin, for his unstoppable love and support for my writing and other creative endeavors, because he knows it makes me happy. Thank you, my love. To my three wonderful sons, Jordan, Joseph and Jacoby; I cannot express how happy, and grateful, I am to have your encouragement and artistic additions to this book to bring my stories to life. Thank you!

I also wish to thank my mother for her examples of extending assist to others in need, and to my father, who demonstrated undiminished love of life, up to his last breath. He taught me the importance of lending a smile and a patient ear to my clients,…which was sometimes all they required to heal themselves.

Contents

Dedication...................................v
Acknowledgments..........................vii

Introduction 1

1   Meet Harry.................................3
2   Why I Do What I Do 11
3   "You Just Shake Off The Dirt, and Climb Back On!"....19
4   When the Horse Says "No."...................23
5   Dog Gone It! 27
6   The Day After..............................30
7   "I'm Just Getting Old." Not!................33
8   Starting - Right - Now! 36
9   Please, Don't Stand On That!................39
10 One Potato 43
11 Two Potato 47
12 Three Potato 51
13 More 57
14 I Don't Want to Look Like That 59
15 Sharpening the Tools: Education And Awareness....65
16 Meet The Parents 70
17 Parental Guidance Recommended 75
18 "Go for The Burn!" Then See Your Physical Therapist....78
19 Enough Said 81

Introduction

When I decided to write this book, it was a natural step from the multiple articles, newsletters, exercise instructions and stories I had already written and shared with my clients. I've always written to encourage clients to actively participate in recovery from whatever ailment brought their path, and mine, together. Many people, including a book editor, suggested I write about my experiences as a physical therapist, as they were both entertaining and instructive. So here at last I've collected these stories into this book, after several years of rewrites, leaving it untouched for extended periods. The writing took a long time due to a combination of my self-consciousness about the relevance of another self-help book, plus the irony of experiencing some of the stories in this book from the other side of the fence. We are never finished learning, are we?

The characters and events portrayed within this book are based on real events.

Yes, really.

My husband asked me this when he was proofreading a section for me. He asked me if these people were real and if they really did do these things that caused injury to themselves. I assured him they were very real. I have changed the names and embellished the situations a bit at times, but overall, there is no limit to the number of ways human beings will cause injury to themselves. It happens daily, without fail, and has kept me in awe of the ability for a human body to not just survive, but to recover and thrive after an injury. And as much as my clients were grateful to me for their healing and recovery, I always made sure they understood that it was their own body that did the healing. I just helped remove some of the obstacles.

Now I'm sharing these stories with you, as I have shared them with my clients through the decades, as part of my continual goal to increase people's awareness of their inner power to heal and be well. It seems most people really do not care to hear about their own pains and the inherent ability to heal themselves; it's much more fun to hear about someone else's struggle to find that power. As Joseph Campbell, so many times related, *"Opportunities to find deeper powers within ourselves come when life seems most challenging."*

Which is why the journey of the hero captures our interest. The Hero of every story overcomes insurmountable odds, unimaginable trials and tribulations. We triumph, as the Hero triumphs within his cause. Even though, what we often don't consciously acknowledge, is how we each carry that hero's heart and abilities to overcome the barriers that appear in our own path.

So, these stories are true, the 'heroes' are real and their abilities to conquer the pain, the frustration and the fatigue which hindered their quests in healing, did happen.

So, let's meet Harry. Because the *cause* of most injuries, are a story within themselves, and may be a lesson worth paying attention to.

CHAPTER 1
Meet Harry

Sharon was a plump and strong-armed fifty-year-old woman who lived by herself on a small Idaho farm, except for a family of animals which she lovingly cared for. The "family" included chickens; multiple dogs for sheepherding, companionship, and hunting; a feral cat with only one purpose (mice); two cows; a horse; a goat; and Harry, the mule.

Sharon had come to me for treatment of severe pain in her right arm and neck that made it almost impossible to lift her hand up far enough to pull a baseball cap over her short, graying hair. She was awkwardly trying to adjust that cap with her left hand as we met in my clinic lobby. The dark green cap, sporting a John Deere logo, skewed sharply to the left, making Sharon look like a gang member from L.A.

This arm pain also interfered with all her home and yard duties, Sharon explained to me, which was more worrisome than the pain itself. She wasn't sure why all the discomfort had occurred, but she did know exactly when it had started.

Harry the Mule ... and Other Injuries

Meet Harry

When Sharon first came to my clinic, it was early August in Southern Idaho, in the middle of a heat wave. This high-desert area reached one-hundred-plus degrees on a daily basis. In the metropolitan area of Boise, most people avoided outdoor activities during the day, whenever possible.

However, Sharon *was* a farmer of sorts, and very concerned for her animals clustered in the dry, dusty corral next to the barn. Those animals bearing their normal heavy coats specifically worried Sharon, including her sheep dog, the goat and, naturally, Harry, the mule. So, Sharon decided, in the name of humanity, not only to cool down these poor, unsuspecting creatures by applying a brisk shower of water from the garden hose, but also—with only the best intentions in her heart—to shave them.

Up to this point in our conversation, I'd been quietly attentive to Sharon, who was now sitting in one of my exam rooms. However, the last remark now had a large red warning flag waving in the back of my brain. The flag was labeled "human versus animal kingdom," with a few alarms ringing, just for effect. YouTube offers multiple stories and videos of people attempting to pet bears at Yellowstone, ride buffalo in Montana, and swim with the fishes (piranha) in the Amazon (South America, not the bargain website). These ventures ended poorly for the people involved. So I, of course, envisioned this burly woman being butted across the yard by the goat, or her arm being wrenched by a kicking mule pulling away from a spray of water.

Curiosity now had me by the ears and stilled my tongue from spewing the multiple questions formulating in my mind. I encouraged her to continue with the story.

As it turned out, the goat named Max, my initial guess for the animal causing Sharon's injury, was easily tethered to a fence and tolerated the bathing and shaving procedure well. Sharon related that Max had been known to stand unperturbed in violent thunderstorms, pelted by hail the size of marbles and blasts of sand thrown about by high winds. As other living creatures ran about seeking shelter, Max would stand amidst all forms of wild elements, his ninja-like jaws snatching snack items swirling around him, like a free buffet, happily chomping away on a mixture of branches, leaves, and Sharon's junk mail.

Sharon's sheep-shearing electric shaver (say *that* three times!) quickly completed the hair-cutting job on Max, and this Zen-like goat wandered off to chew on some weeds near the corner of the house.

The sheepdog was next in line to be sheared. Not being an actual sheep, he was tolerant of the garden-hose shower, but less cooperative when the shears began buzzing near his head.

"I had to give him a bit of a headlock to get the job done," Sharon said, describing her technique, "but he was fine once I finished."

Although he was visibly cooler, per Sharon's description, the canine quickly hid in naked shame under the porch steps, glaring at her in indignation.

By this point, Sharon reported, she had been at this task of barnyard savior for over three hours, and she was, admittedly, "a bit tired." Although the sun was high in the sky and the temperature had soared from early-morning seventy degrees to a blistering hundred-and-one, Sharon was not one to shy away from hard work of any kind. She pressed on, restarting the entire process on Harry the Mule.

She reached for the garden hose, hoping the initial watering-down of this large beast would be enough for the day, as they both were feeling the August heat. She turned on the hose, moving around him briskly and adjusting the spray settings to achieve the highest benefit. Although he bravely and stoically stood his ground in the now very muddy corral, Harry was, well, hairy.

It was now just past midday, with the oven-hot air almost immediately drying Harry's drenched, shaggy coat. Sharon watched in frustration as the briefly cooling water now began steaming upward in visible lines of vapor, practically parboiling Harry in the process.

She recounted his large head hanging in the relentless heat as he stood in a puddle of mud, his large brown eyes staring expectantly upward at her. He looked pitiful, and Sharon truly felt sorry for him. So she moved him to a dry section of the corral, took the electric shaver in hand once more, and started to laboriously sweep the razor over Harry's hairy hide. She started at his neck, carefully folding his long, rabbit-like ears forward to avoid clipping them, then moved the razor over his shoulders and front legs. Over and over and over—a hundred times or more—Sharon's now-sunburned right arm swept the razor across Harry, removing large tufts of hair, which floated to the ground and began to pile around her work boots.

Why only the right arm, you may ask? A fair question, which I posed to Sharon at this point, beginning to suspect the source of the pain that had brought her to my clinic.

"Well," she responded, as if I were asking the most obvious question in the world, "because I'm right-handed, of course!"

Of course. And to this Idahoan, as to many people working with any handheld equipment needing focus and coordination, switching hands periodically simply didn't occur to her. Or, for that matter, even make sense. I started to say so when Sharon continued her story.

She managed to shave all the way past Harry's ribs, continuing with vigorous sweeps of the razor. Then, to her surprise, her right arm suddenly and completely went "dead," as she described it.

The still-buzzing razor fell from her hand into the dirt at her feet, sending up a big poof of dust and mule hair.

Sharon stared at the dropped razor.

She stared at her half-shaved mule.

And, knowing the job was only half done, she knew she absolutely had to continue in spite of her numb arm. Yet as she bent to pick up the razor, she could not convince her fingers to once more curl around the tool. Heck, she couldn't even feel her hand! Everything from her armpit to her fingertips was totally numb.

In my exam room, Sharon now leaned forward intensely.

"I could see my arm," she said, jabbing her thick left index finger at her right bicep, "but it was just hanging there, like it was someone else's!" She released a big sigh and leaned back in her chair. "That really scared me!"

At this point in her recital, she looked at me directly. True sadness was reflected in her eyes. I waited for her to say that this fear of losing movement and feeling in her arm prompted her to seek medical attention. However, she slowly shook her head, drawing a deep, shaky breath.

"Poor Harry!" she finally blurted out, tears in her voice. "He's still out there!" She sighed. "He's out there in this horrible heat, only half-shaved!" She sighed again, her pale blue eyes starting to fill with tears, threatening to spill over at any moment.

(Incidentally, I hate this part, when people are on the edge of crying. It makes my eyes tear up in sympathy. No stopping it.)

Meet Harry

But then, to my surprise, Sharon unexpectedly added, "Harry's *ass* must be so hot!"

I paused for a moment as my imagination took over, picturing the long, sad face of a mule, the big, dark-brown eyes full of tears (like his owner seated in front of me), his shaggy hind-end in sharp contrast to his clean-shaven front half. A cross between a centaur and a victim of Puck from *A Midsummer Night's Dream*, standing in a dusty corral, suffering in the relentless heat of the Idaho summer sun.

It was too much, and I burst out laughing.

Luckily, after only a brief, startled pause, Sharon joined me in some much-needed laughter.

When we had both recovered our composure, Sharon wiped the mixed tears of sadness and silliness from her eyes, and I resumed my professional (well, mostly) demeanor. Still smiling, I proceeded to explain to this big-hearted farmgirl how the events she'd just described led up to her numb arm and stiff neck. I summarized that five hours of innumerable repetitive shaving movements with her right arm absolutely fatigued her muscles. The muscles then spasmed, pinching off the blood supply to the controlling nerves. *This* is what had forced the arm to stop working. Numbness is a natural response of the body to being overworked, and its way of protecting itself from further injury.

I then leaned toward Sharon and looked her in the eye, wanting her full attention. I reminded this farmgirl that it was also natural to let animals deal with nature's heat in their own manner, including sweating a bit under all their fur.

She looked a bit embarrassed, then laughed again, nodding. After a little more education about her own body and how she'd probably ignored some early signs of impending muscle fatigue, she agreed she may have pushed herself. Not an easy admission for an independent gal like Sharon.

Luckily, after a couple weeks of treatment, Sharon was close to a full recovery. She happily resumed all her normal work on the farm, caring for all her animals just as she had before the injury, with a few recommended changes from me, her physical therapist.

A couple months later, Sharon emailed me a thank-you. Included was a photo of her beloved Harry, now fully shaved, of course, looking as content as a mule could be.

I may be mistaken, but he looked like he was smiling.

CHAPTER 2

Why I Do What I Do

I AM A PHYSICAL THERAPIST.
I have made the interesting choice to work in a medical profession known for the dichotomy of both the alleviation *and* the infliction of pain. I have made a steady effort over the past three decades to change this latter concept. Who wants to be known as a "physical terrorist?"

In order to change people's initial expectations of physical therapy, I've used a balance of compassion and education in determining what their body needs to heal. My approach to support healing is not considered 'usual', as I allowed the time to listen, and *validate*, each client's pain and limitations. So many people hesitate to seek any assistance in healing, because they feel like they shouldn't be complaining at all. Therefore, the most important task I make sure to assist them with is reducing their pain as quickly as possible. Which gains a measure of trust.

This base of trust then supports the progressive layers of knowledge which I then add to throughout each session. I help each client better understand their body, cause of injury and thus reduce future chances of injury.

Hopefully.

Unfortunately, I must concede that without the pain, most people would not bother to pass the threshold of my clinic door.

My philosophy is not only based on preventing more pain as I treat, but also allowing each person to participate as fully as possible in their recovery. I honestly believe all individuals should know how to take care of this wonderful "gift" of nature: their bodies.

This is important to remember: *We are each responsible for these 'gifts,' our bodies, 24/7!*

"No pain? Great!" is patients' initial response when I present my general philosophy of pain-free recovery. "All for it!"

However, many folks are reluctant to take on the aforementioned responsibility involved. That's because I ask each person to *think* before they act, to be sure they will not be causing further injury to themselves. *Thinking* is the last thing people want to do as they dash around to complete life's little chores.

Of course, they *are* thinking about something—just not about what they are doing *now*.

For example, in your mind, you might be three or four errands ahead of your present task of, for instance, chopping vegetables in the kitchen. As you wield the sharp Ginsu knife with one hand, the fingers of the other hand are lining up the carrots to be sliced for stew. The knife starts slicing carrots into nice, precise sizes, but then your brain shifts to driving the car to pick up the kids from school. Or folding laundry. Or any other multiple tasks you need to do next.

The Treadmill of Life is going, so run, run, run as fast as you can!

The problem is, you *are* actually still chopping vegetables with your hands. But your brain is now only attending twenty- to thirty percent to the knife placement. That's because you have also tasked your brain to guide your hands in holding the car's steering wheel fifteen minutes from now. So you most likely will get a nasty cut on that left index finger. Why? Because your body thinks it's making the left-hand turn into the school driveway at the same time you pull the knife across a carrot, but did not move your finger in time in order to avoid hitting the curb.

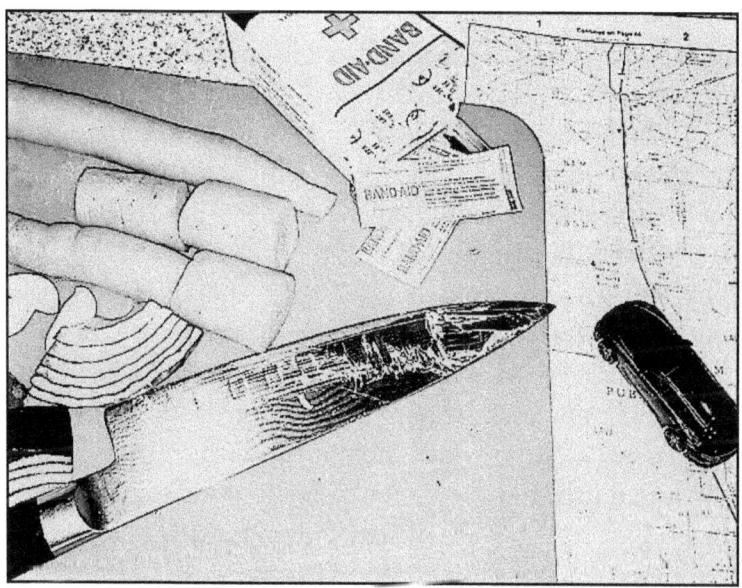

Confused? So is the body.

The reason is simple: there is no such thing as "multitasking."

Research shows the brain works only on *one thing at a time*. When you are juggling tasks, such as eating a sandwich, watching TV and reading the newspaper, the brain places two of these items on stand-by in order to work on the one of choice.

The better your brain is at switching between these tasks while providing sufficient focus to do the task well, (like taking a bite of sandwich and not your fingers), the more it feels like you are getting multiple things done at once. However, have you ever eaten a sandwich and not really remembered what it tasted like? Maybe not all of the task was captured by the brain. And it is often the case that it still takes forty-five minutes to do three fifteen-minute jobs.

So what I am trying to teach my clients is that when you are completing an activity—any activity—pay attention fully to what you are asking your body to do. The *Zen* of injury prevention, so to speak, relies strongly on an individual's willingness to learn *Body-Awareness*.

I often force-feed individuals on the first visit, bombarding them with vital knowledge in self-care. I try my best to get their thoughts focused on the *now*—"what are you doing *now*"— and, Heaven forbid, ask them to acknowledge what they *feel*! Many people hate to admit they have any pain, unless they are practically writhing on the floor. They may drag a sprained ankle into my clinic, but when asked to tell me about their pain, they initially try to deny it's actually "pain" they feel. So I inevitably meet with resistance to all my outlandish, foo-foo, "touchy-feely" stuff of listening to the body's messages. People are convinced that the idea that self-awareness can promote self-healing "just can't be right!"

"My body should just take care of itself!" is the indignant reply to my suggestions. "I shouldn't be bothered by these aches and pains!" and, inevitably, "It was never a problem when I was young!"

Ah. And now onto aging, a process most folks believe they have no control over.

Let's examine that falsehood of "I am getting older, therefore I will hurt," because there are many facets contributing to all these semi-myths.

Deepak Chopra is a well regarded medical physician who has dedicated his career to the phenomenon called the *Mind-Body Connection*. He made the following statement regarding our ability to either block or support self-healing, which is a cornerstone to avoid being in chronic pain: "One of the unique things about the human brain is that it can do only what it thinks it can do. The minute you say 'My memory isn't what it used to be' or 'I can't remember a thing today,' you are actually training your brain to live up to your diminished expectations."

Diminished expectations? Ouch! I don't know about you, but I don't usually get up in the morning and decide to have a less-than-great day. However, many people preface their abilities, or lack thereof, with "I can't."

Dr. Chopra also said, "No matter how much it gets abused, the body can restore balance. The first rule is to stop interfering with nature. … A gentle focus of attention is all it takes to free the body of minor imbalances."

No control over our aging, or our state of health? Extensive research has shown this is the furthest from the truth. And it's not just about eating right, not smoking, and getting exercise. How you *think* affects how you *heal*.

We *do* have the power over how we age and *if* we will be in pain.

Now before all this serious talk continues to decline into a lecture, let me introduce my most powerful ally: humor.

I have asked myself this question daily: "What would I do without the stress-reducing power of laughter?" Most likely

I'd hang up my physical-therapy license and work as a barista. However, as I have been successfully helping people undo the damage and pain they have presented to me for over thirty years—and can still laugh—I suppose the coffee industry will be safe for a while.

Despite my joking teasing and play on words, I never lose sight of the fact that my patients' lives have been interrupted by their debilities. Validation of their pain and resulting limitations requires an attentive audience. Otherwise, they would not be sitting in my clinic or listening to my "sage" professional advice. The tough part is always convincing a new client that they really can go through treatment ... and life ... much more comfortably, if they choose to.

"No pain, no gain!" is the inevitable saying thrown at me within the first ten to twenty minutes of meeting a new client. But even as they utter that familiar yet demoralizing statement, equating pain with healing, they are hoping I have some instant cure up my sleeve. Maybe an extra-special exercise, or perhaps a magic wand! Yes! Then I could just wave it dramatically over them, muttering something like "Bibbity, bobbity, boo!" and make all their troubles go away.

That would be great! Even I think so.

As it is, I actually *do* have a magic wand. On one end is a gold sparkling star, attached to a long handle. I picked it up at a dollar store and placed it on the wall of my treatment room. There is even a sign beneath it that reads, "For Emergency Use Only."

Of course, each person who spots that wand feels that their pain or ailment constitutes an "emergency." I admit, the wand has become a sneaky way to lead conversations toward the discovery of who is really responsible for an individual's health and wellness.

"Do you know the secret as to how this problem is going to be healed?" I say to my unsuspecting client. They lean forward expectantly, all attention focused on this soon-to-be-shared revelation.

"*You* are going to heal this problem," I say, watching a look of skepticism form on the client's face, "because ninety percent of getting better depends on what you do and don't do once you leave my office."

A spark of hope shows in their eyes. True, they are still uncertain, but then I explain that my real skills lie in removing obstacles to healing. I help control the swelling, the muscle tightness, and of course, the pain. Plus, I offer constant education in injury prevention.

I explain that I can remove obstacles, but the actual healing process is done by the person's body, not me. Nothing magical about it, really. The greatest obstacle I am trying to remove is created by their own beliefs and disbeliefs about healing and aging.

"Knowledge is the first step to health," I tell them. Over and over again, I state this.

Yet no matter how well I coax, train, calm, and remove the physical obstacles toward healing, the greatest barrier to a quick return to health remains the person themselves.

That "No Pain, No Gain!" philosophy is so engrained in each member of our society that it overwhelms common sense, as well as any attempts their body makes to communicate which actions or habits are helpful, and which are harmful.

The first step is to stop interfering with nature. I have a big job ahead of me, guiding each client through this maze of new ideas and then teaching them how to apply them to their lives. *They* have the choice of how much suffering they will endure, now and in the future.

Call me a radical (many do!) because I want to change the way people treat themselves, allowing them a chance to go through life as pain-free as possible. I do this one person at a time, one day at a time ... and I love it.

I believe it can be done. Each time I see this new awareness blossom in another client, when I witness that *aha!* moment, I feel a satisfaction in my work, knowing one more person has found the miracle to heal within themselves. That's an internal magic wand they can take anywhere!

Thankfully, most of my clients make this choice by the time they leave my care, educated and willing to pay better attention to their body's needs. Even better, I see parents share with children, husbands with wives, and I feel hope that this increased knowledge is helping the next generation become a little more healthy. At least, that's the plan.

"Listen carefully," I tell them, "to the small messages of tiredness or tension, when the body is speaking softly. Don't wait for the message to get louder and louder, essentially yelling for help. Because that is what pain is: a warning signal we should not ignore."

Okay, so I just relayed my real message of this book in the initial two chapters. However, this book is also about sharing some of my adventures, such as they are, in my world of medicine.

So, what else comes through my door? Read on! And remember, laughter *is* the greatest healer of all.

CHAPTER 3

"You Just Shake Off The Dirt, and Climb Back On!"

Living in Idaho, we see horse owners practically on every corner. And there are many types of equestrian facilities to accommodate the various uses humans have for horses.

Some horses are pets, cared for by the kids for basic recreation and 4-H projects. Others are very highly bred and trained for show and competition, living a somewhat pampered, though controlled, life. And of course, there are the work horses, used on farms and ranches to help in the daily chores.

It is an interesting arrangement, as horses naturally view humans as predators. Historically our ancestors used them for food as well as transportation. But somehow, various partnerships between humans and horses have developed over thousands of years.

Horses are intelligent, sturdy, strong, and hardworking team members in all these instances. However, they are just as temperamental and moody as you and I, with individual personalities. Meaning they can be very sweet, or very mean. It just may depend on the day, and which side of the stall they wake up on.

A number of individuals that come through my clinic door have been injured by horses. But in some cases they were already sporting some kind of stiffness or muscle restriction before the horse had its turn at them. Often this initial muscle limitation was exacerbated by swinging a leg over the saddle, or bouncing in a trot too roughly.

But when some riders tell me what occurred in other horse-related incidents, well, let's just say I am surprised their owners survived the event at all, much less have the physical ability to come in and tell me about it. The list includes being thrown onto rocks; stepped on, kicked in the knee, back and head; dragged, head-butted and bitten; or, any combination of these dire events.

I had to get used to hearing some pretty traumatic stories while examining bruised and twisted bodies.

The responses of the riders, however, were even more astonishing to get used to—a sort of "Oh, well" attitude. "This kind of stuff just happens with horses." And the injury was not going to stop the rider from getting on a horse again.

Initially I was confused as to why horse-riding was such a passion. Personally, I am not particularly inclined to come within ten feet of a horse. I would feel safer standing right next to a loaded cannon.

No matter how battered the rider was, they told me time and again, that this was how it was with horses. When I would recommend a rest from riding to speed the healing, they would plead, "Please, doctor!" (I often had to remind clients that I was not a physician, but they still called me doctor.) "Please, doctor, get me well enough to ride, as soon as possible!" The plea was heartfelt, but seemed almost obsessive to me, the non-horse-lover.

Hmmm. I had to step back and try to look at the whole picture.

These folks had large bruises, wrenched limbs and spines, head injuries and other assorted wounds—injuries usually reserved for car accidents and misfortunes involving large machinery. But, horses *are* very large, and very powerful, just like some dangerous machinery.

Unlike machines, however, they are also greatly loved and cherished by their owners. Horses become part of the family. Not to mention the vast amount of money and time invested in these beloved horses, the importance of which was not lost on me.

I finally recognized that keeping and riding horses was a choice in lifestyle, just like practicing yoga, driving trucks, making do-it-yourself home repairs (another chapter on this one), and tinkering with old cars. Keeping horses reflected a choice in hobbies, vocations, and beliefs. *This* is what made them happy.

I spoke of this mindset among horse-people and was referred to sports therapist Seana Adamson, who lives in California. Seana teaches equestrian riding during the day. At night she counsels distressed riders who are attempting a return to the saddle after an "incident" that has forced them out.

In my phone interview with Seana, she agreed that horses and people may have been drawn to each other over the centuries. However, since every horse is different, the rider should closely observe how a horse behaves in a herd of other horses. That behavior is an indication of how the horse will behave with the rider.

Consider the physical pushing, kicking, and nipping that occurs in a horse's social norm for discipline and play. What one horse does physically with another horse as play could *kill* a human.

Plus, Seana added, we have bred specific horses for specific activities such as show-riding, pleasure riding, and farming. This breeding has included increased intelligence, which can create both good and bad outcomes.

According to Seana, sometimes a person really does need to be afraid of a particular horse that may not meet their needs.

"That relationship must end," she emphasized, "for the safety of the rider, and move on to a horse that can get along better with humans."

Good advice, I think.

Whether to return to the mental and physical challenges of riding after an injury remains fully the client's own choice—a choice I have learned to respect. If possible, I help my client achieve the expected return to the saddle, no matter how I inwardly cringe, imagining the next incident that would bring them to my door.

At least they come to *my* door.

CHAPTER 4

When the Horse Says "No."

HERE IS SOME HORSE-OWNER wisdom which I feel impelled to share.

A horse says no when, at a full gallop, it plants all four legs in a sudden stop to let you enjoy the sensation of sailing through thin air. All because a tumbleweed rolled into its path.

A horse says no because you paid too much attention to the horse in the other corral first. When you finally come over to share a carrot, he nips you as a way of saying, "Don't forget … I am the most important one here!" (My own interpretation … I don't really speak horse.)

A horse says no when she is tired, or ill, and therefore resists movement. This is reminiscent of a human toddler who will whine and slump to the ground, challenging you to drag her through a grocery store while other parents smile in understanding … a look that says, "Been there, done that." However, a thousand-pound horse is hard to drag anywhere, so she generally will get her way and not do too much.

And yes, horses have been known to whine and slump to the ground, as well.

A horse says no when a wasp buzzes its ear while it's prancing to its rider's command. Precision footwork now becomes the dance-of-the-possessed, as the horse bucks and twists to get away from the offending insect.

Unfortunately, the person seated on the horse's back, supposedly in control, has now been thrown into a wooden wall, all the air expelled from her lungs. Plus, not so conveniently, said rider is now sporting a few wooden slivers in her backside. So much for dancing with your partner!

Harry the Mule ... and Other Injuries

CHAPTER 5

Dog Gone It!

The destructive force of man's best friend has never ceased to amaze me. How our canine friends are capable of inflicting injury on their owners is not limited to biting the hand that feeds them.

We love our dogs, another animal welcomed into the family. Dogs are great companions through thick and thin, until they act like, well, dogs.

The canine brain is triggered by primitive instincts, like "Squirrel!" or cat, or bird, or whatever offending lesser creature has entered the vision of our canine walking partner. And then this domesticated pal of man (or woman) goes into full alert!

The hair raises on the nape of its neck, the tail curls up like an antenna and the wolf is unleashed from within. The chase is on! The need to dominate prevails!

This transformation all happens in a millisecond, with the unsuspecting owner—you—still attached on the other end of the leash, and now becoming a casualty of this predator display.

The squirrel now stops in its tracks, squaring off with the dog, nose twitching and tail flicking in nervous agitation. The squirrel makes its move, faking to the left and then the right. The dog is now jumping side to side, barking, with its head lowered to keep an eye on its prey.

You now find that the long leash, so helpful in letting your dog roam farther, is now wrapping around your legs as the two animals jockey for position. The squirrel dashes to the nearest tree, inconveniently behind you.

The dog immediately darts in hot pursuit of its prey, the tangled leash yanked taut against your legs. The legs snap together in a decidedly awkward and unbalanced stance. Checkmate.

Your hobbled feet are pulled briskly out from underneath your teetering form and then, in a grand, majestic arc of flailing limbs, you are dumped squarely onto the dirt (or concrete or gravel. No matter. They all hurt on impact.)

If this has ever happened to you, the first thing you may notice is where the squirrel ended up. You see it laughing and chittering in victory, high above your head. It sits comfortably on a branch within the sanctuary of a tree, supposedly "captured" by your loving dog.

Luckily, you don't have to move a muscle to have a great view of the offending squirrel, since moving at all is unlikely. *Everything* hurts.

Ultimately, despite your present painful situation, you are much more embarrassed, even mortified, that your neighbors may have seen the entire event unfold. Perhaps you manage a quick flick of the eyes side to side, checking your surroundings for witnesses. Which is all you can physically manage anyways, in your present, uh, "altered" condition.

Oh, no! Mrs. Potts is out watering her dahlias! The local news station might as well be filming this, if *she* saw anything!

Strange how you worry about what the neighbors will think, even as you struggle to suck in life-giving breath, the fall having knocked the wind out of you.

You gasp, trying all the while to give Mrs. Potts the impression that you meant to lay here all along. Maybe you manage a weak wave, giving a meaningful look up at the clouds and birds, all the while noting that your left leg is trapped in a not-so-comfortable angle from the taut leash your dog continues to tug at.

This loving dog finally returns to your prostrate form, smiling down at you, panting doggie-breath in your face and drooling in contentment.

Good dog.

CHAPTER 6

The Day After

In my clinic, the conversation usually goes like this: "*How did you twist your back, Mrs. Jones?... Oh! Oh, my! So, your dog cut you off at the knees while jogging because she started chasing a stray cat across the street?... Yes, I'm sure those large scabs on your kneecaps will heal eventually. Good thing you had those crutches at home so you could make your appointment today.*"

Several of my slight-of-build and, unfortunately, older clients have been thrown unceremoniously to the ground by a sudden jerk on the leash: swept off their feet, so to speak, as their "sweet and gentle" Great Dane or one-hundred-pound Golden Lab leaps ahead to *protect* their owner.

Dogs also seem to enjoy dashing headlong into their owner's knees in bursts of affection, pushing joints in a different direction than nature intended.

Most often, however, the most painful dog injuries have occurred from the Pekinese named "Lola" or "Fluffy" who needs a boost onto the bed or into the car, or whom their owner just wants to pick up to cuddle.

Although Fluffy weighs only ten pounds (a bit chubby for a Pekinese), Mrs. Smith's upper body weighs eighty pounds. Because Mrs. Smith doesn't bend her knees to squat as she scoops up Fluffy, she is now lifting ninety pounds. Why? When leaning forward at the waist, knees straight as table legs, your body weight is now outside the normal base of support for your spine, which is the hips and pelvis. So the spine now has to pick up ninety pounds all by itself.

How often do you, my reader, pick up ninety pounds?

The strain to the spine itself is actually much more than ninety pounds. Doctors and scientists have measured the pressures in the vertebral discs using needles. (Ow!) However, the physics are too much for this book to list the involved angles, vectors, and calculus.

Trust me.

1. FACE YOUR LOAD.
2. FEET APART.
3. BEND YOUR KNEES.
4. HOLD THE LOAD CLOSE TO YOUR BELLY BUTTON.
5. DON'T TWIST AS YOU LIFT.
6. MOVE YOUR FEET TO TURN.

Six simple steps. That's really all it takes to help with safe lifting.

Anyway, back to Mrs. Smith and the result of her straight-legged doggie lift. In making that small, low-to-the-ground movement of lifting her dog, Mrs. Smith's back is now injured. Now she finds she can't pick up a napkin or put on her socks, much less pick up Fluffy.

Poor Fluffy.

Harry the Mule ... and Other Injuries

CHAPTER 7

"I'm Just Getting Old." Not!

A GREAT DEAL OF MY lengthy career in physical therapy has been dedicated toward the education of the hapless "victims" of back pain. It just doesn't make sense to most individuals that something so simple as picking up a pencil from the floor should have "thrown out" their backs. It's sometimes difficult to convince someone that it was the first *one hundred* "pencils" picked up while bending incorrectly that have led to this present painful condition.

The proverbial last-straw effect of pencil number one-hundred-and-one is when the back has said, "I can't do this anymore!" and now has the full attention of the abuser.

Of course, it's nothing *they* did, my patients lament. It's the weather, the stress in their lives, and ultimately, their *age*! Any and all external factors are thrown into the pot of blame, with age inevitably making the top of the list.

So when the "victim" enters my clinic and utters those all-so-familiar words in a defeated voice, "I'm just getting old," much to their surprise, I immediately tell them the following:

"We don't use the 'age card' around here. It's *mileage,* not age, that caused your problem."

"Huh?" They look stunned at my apparent lack of respect for my elders.

"Besides," I add as their mouths drop open, "I can't fix age. If someone is convinced their problem is fully due to age, how in the world can I possibly make a difference?"

As I pose this question to them, the lights start to go on. One, there is hope. Two, their minds are suddenly opened to another way of thinking.

Certainly, there are age-related changes in our bodies that we cannot ignore. We do have chemical and hormonal changes that reduce the springiness and endurance of our youth. And over the years, our bodies' cells don't repair at the speed of light, as when we were teenagers.

However, after I have acknowledged the obvious age changes, I emphasize to my clients that we still have the capacity *to repair damage! We* do *heal, and we* do *continue to make new cells* daily*!*

If we did not complete daily repair and make new cells for those regularly damaged pieces, we would be on our way out. In other words, we would be *dead*!

Now *that* gets their attention!

On a daily basis, our body is cleaning house of poorly working or injured cells. Plus, we injure and destroy thousands of cells in our bodies simply through normal, everyday activities. That bite of food that traveled down your throat at lunch crushed and injured a bunch of cells on its journey to your gut.

But have no fear! Your body is designed to handle all these injuries and *will* fix them. Plenty more where that came from! That's because we make new building blocks all the time. Just make sure that the food you just swallowed was filled with the right nutrition to make those replacement parts.

The amazing abilities of our bodies to heal and repair themselves, each and every day, continues on, no matter how many years you pile on.

When I said "mileage" was more to blame than age, this relates to the use and abuse that has occurred over the lifetime of the owner, no matter how young or old we may be. It also takes into account how well we've repaired and recovered from previous injuries and past diseases, as well as what health issues we are dealing with now.

It's cumulative. One incident builds upon the next, and the body records these incidents within your inner medical history file. There's no going back to the day you were born to undo all those injuries from falls out of trees, sports, or work strains. Let's add the moments of cigarette, alcohol, and drug abuse too, which create wrecking-ball-like tissue breakdown. There was that bout with pneumonia, the flu, or the diabetes that developed in adulthood. All we can do is move forward, make healthier choices, and assist our bodies to heal.

CHAPTER 8

Starting - Right - Now!

Not tomorrow, not after the recent crisis or next relationship problem is resolved. Now!

Because, there will always be a drama that threatens to overwhelm us, and by proactively improving our health choices, those dramas will be weathered with less physical damage.

So, back to Mrs. Smith's injured back, and Fluffy.

Yes, Fluffy. Because that dog is still there, underfoot and needing food, potty time outside, and love. How can Mrs. Smith ever recover if Fluffy remains in the picture, tempting her to bend over yet again and again?

Mrs. Smith can learn new tricks, even at seventy-five years of age.

Tools and accessories are available to help her, such as lightweight steps that enable dogs to climb up onto the bed and into the car. Mrs. Smith can learn how to bend her knees, or to sit down before reaching to the floor and lifting Fluffy for a cuddle, thus reducing the stress to her spine.

While Mrs. Smith is recovering from her injury, she can ask for assistance from family and friends to walk Fluffy or to buy dog food. Maybe even make her a sandwich while they are at it, right?

Believe it or not, this is the hardest trick for adults to learn: asking for help. Nearly everyone I make this suggestion to—"ask for help"—comes back at me and exclaims, " I just can't impose on anyone else. My family is way too busy!"

However, when I turn the question around and ask, "Wouldn't you help someone if *they* asked?" they inevitably respond with, "Why, of course!"

We all *need* help sometimes, and we all *give* help sometimes. That's why we even bother to live in a community, not alone in a shack, out in the deepest part of the woods.

So ASK FOR HELP! Someone is waiting to help you. I guarantee it.

CHAPTER 9

Please, Don't Stand On That!

Funny how human beings, and goats, seem to believe they have the ability to stand on any and all items. Granted, we have all seen acrobats, gymnasts and the occasional toddler, succeeding at feats of unimaginable balance. Unfortunately, the majority of attempts by the rest of us to demonstrate higher levels of coordination, result in not so graceful, or pain free, outcomes.

I remember one particular morning, as I worked in a hospital setting, chatting with a neurosurgeon. I remarked that he looked 'rather haggard' in his appearance, mentally noting the hair sticking up at all angles on one side of his head, while the hair on the other side was flattened against his skull. Extreme bed hair. Poor sleep, emphasized by the dark circles under his eyes.

The neurosurgeon sighed and let me know he was performing hours of spinal surgery on a college kid until a couple hours ago, trying to ensure the young man would walk again after a bad fall off a fraternity house roof. The doctor then remarked, "Most of these accidents begin with, 'Here,...hold my beer and watch this!' The surgeon's shoulders slumped a little more. "I really hate those two a.m. calls from E.R," he finished, giving another tired sigh. Then he shuffled off to finish his morning rounds.

Human beings,...and goats. A goal for a goat that wanders up to an elevated surface may be to look for food, seek safety from predators, or attain a good viewpoint to search for the latter. Humans also have some kind of goal in mind when we plan our ascent to higher peaks. Logically, we tell ourselves, "Yes. I can clean the top of the refrigerator, if I just had something to step up on." We look quickly left and right, because we are inherently too lazy to go out to the garage and get the step stool we just picked up at the local hardware store.

So, what is within a few feet of the fridge? Well, - there's pull-out drawers shelving in the cupboards, the inside of the fridge itself, (Of course, only after you put a clean towel down on the glass shelving to step on.). Maybe, an upside-down cooking pot? However, everyone's all-time favorite seems to be the kitchen chair.

Now, this seems like a good idea, with four sturdy legs and all. Yet, the base of chairs is not built for uneven pressure. It relies on our bottoms to be firmly settled on the seat to keep the chair legs balanced on the floor. Plus, the average seat height is 17 inches. Quite a high first step for shorter folks to be attempting. So, what happens when we do manage to crawl up and place all of our body weight on that chair, balancing on only our two feet? It's ok for standing absolutely still with even weight and flat feet. However, we are *cleaning,* right? Scrubbing, reaching with determined vigor, and nothing is escaping the cleaning rag wiping that dusty, dirty fridge top.

A quick, big lean to get the back corner, achieved by shifting all the weigh to the right foot, up on tippy toe,....and Presto! Now, the chair tips up sharply on two legs.

Let's pause right there. So many options to describe at this point. Actually, let's ask a couple more questions first. Such as, are you in stocking feet? (Extra slippery surface). Are there wheels on the chair legs? (Extra, extra slippery). Finally, are you a gymnast? Or a goat?

Because once a chair tips, gravity and physics will take over, creating a rapid landslide effect. Everybody off!

Humans have an amazing built-in mechanism to maintain balance, called the vestibular system, which we utilize daily to walk, put our pants on and climb upon chairs. When the proverbial rug is pulled out from underneath us, reflexes kick in and we begin to throw our weight in various directions in an attempt to correct the sudden loss of footing. It is not a pretty sight, with most results involving unsightly bruises, sprained limbs and the occasional broken bone.

So, what if you had grabbed the step stool from the garage? Unfortunately, although step stools and ladders are designed for standing on, you are still limited in reaching to the sides. Get off the ladder, shift it to better alignment with your task, and save yourself the misery of an urgent care visit, where they will ask you to share your story. Because someone, *me*,…will then write about it.

Harry the Mule ... and Other Injuries

CHAPTER 10

One Potato …

"So, Molly, you say you twisted your ankle while hanging up a picture?"

"Well, yes, but it was on the wall, above my headboard. You see"— Molly carefully moves her swollen ankle into a different position—"I've had this pretty painting sitting off in a corner for months, because Edgar, my husband, said he'd take care of hanging it right away."

"But," I interject, "you've been waiting 'months,' so you thought you would take care of it on your own, and—"

"Right!" Molly jumps back in to her explanation. "And you know, Edgar gets so busy, and I thought I just needed to hammer in a nail and that it would be a quick thing to do while he was out in the yard spraying weeds." Molly takes a deep breath, then rushes on. "There are so many dandelions this year, aren't there?"

"Yes, there are," I agree, thinking of my own yellow-covered lawn. Then I prompt my client to clarify what I already suspected.

"So, Molly," I casually ask, "what did you stand on while hammering this nail into the wall above your headboard?"

There is a long silence as Molly lowers her eyes to the floor.

"Oh," she finally says, her high voice wavering a little nervously, "I just climbed up on the bed, because I was having a good day. I mean, my arthritis wasn't bothering my knee." She touches her left knee meaningfully. "And it was only for a minute!" Molly finishes in a rush, lifting her head to look at me.

"Did you lose your balance and fall off the bed?" I quietly question, keeping my voice as neutral and nonjudgmental as possible. Except my brain keeps flashing images of seventy-seven-year-old Molly flailing her arms wildly as she falls through the air.

"Heavens, no!" Her voice is now somewhat defensive. I inwardly begin a sigh of relief, until she clarifies by saying, "I *jumped* off."

Molly is now smiling beautifully at the shocked look on my face.

"Jumped?" I repeat stupidly.

"Yep!" Definitely pleased with herself now. "You know, I used to do gymnastics back in high school."

My mind interjects silently that this was over fifty years ago, but I remain silent as she continues.

"And I would have landed it free and clear if my crocheted blanket hadn't tangled over my left foot."

I am only able to raise my eyebrows at this point, keeping my lips pressed together to avoid letting the unprofessional exclamation from slipping out.

Molly continues. "So, because of that blanket, I did twist my right ankle when I landed." She lifts her right foot and pulls back her pant leg, exposing more of the black-and-blue bruising peeking over her sneaker top. I nod my head to acknowledge her explanation, my hands itching to start actual treatment to reduce all that swelling spilling over her tight anklets. However, she has not finished her story yet, so I smile and simply write *extensive hematoma* on my clipboard.

Molly makes an additional comment that snaps my head up from writing. "And I kind of bounced off the dresser with my shoulder, but I didn't *fall!*" She is almost indignant in her recital, and she looks at me defiantly.

I smile.

Molly smiles.

Then I congratulate Molly for not breaking any bones, and calmly suggest she never do that again. I proceed to examine the swollen and bruised ankle, then the shoulder she "bounced" off of.

CHAPTER 11

Two Potato ...

GEORGE, A GROUCHY EIGHTY-YEAR-OLD with a dry sense of humor, comes banging through the front door of my clinic one day, dragging his left leg along behind him. The lobby is, thankfully, empty at the moment, as he loudly announces, "I just fell on my damned ass." He pauses long enough to grab the front of his trouser leg to pull his left leg closer. "And now I can't move my leg!"

George is moderately stooped in posture from arthritis and peers up at me through his gray shaggy eyebrows. Our eyes lock as I size up the situation in front of me. He may have once stood taller than my five foot nine inches, but George's life "mileage" has added up, and I am definitely towering over this grizzled ex-truck driver.

"Think it's broke?" he finally asks, leaning heavily on the reception-window counter to avoid placing pressure on the left leg.

George is what we call a "repeat offender," meaning he gets injured, gets well, and then repeats the injury, as in this scenario. George had previously injured the same leg trying to simultaneously carry a bag of groceries and walk his dog. See the previous chapter to learn how combinations like that end up.

This time, George explains, he was fixing the drapes in his office. I carefully assist him to a reception room chair, firmly holding his left arm while pulling the chair up behind him to prevent any attempt to throw himself the distance. Not that this impulsive man would do that, right?

I pull up another chair to face him directly.

"What were you standing on, George, to reach up so high?"

"Just a chair."

"What kind of chair?"

"Well …." The hesitation tells me everything, "The one I sit on at my desk," he snaps. I give him a reproachful look, as I don't let people be rude to me, especially when asking me for help. He lowers his eyes, and his attitude. "The drapes are on the window above my desk," he mumbles.

"Oh?" I let the question hang to allow him the chance to tell me what really happened. George likes to leave out details of his injuries.

"Yeah. They weren't closing all the way and the light was bugging my eyes, so I stood on my desk chair."

"A desk chair with wheels?" I hold my breath, but already know the answer by the look in his eyes. It's the same look a child gives you when you catch them with flammable material and matches.

"Uh, yeah. And, well … it slipped out from under me, landing me right on my ass!" George blurts out again. "Hurt like hell, but I managed to get up after a minute."

"Then, you came here?" I asked, truly amazed he could get up after a fall. George is not a spry man, and I was still contemplating the logistics of getting him out of the solid reception chair.

"Hell, no!" He fidgets in his seat to offset pressure from his left hip. "I still had to fix that damned drape, so I just climbed right back up on that chair. Oh!" he quickly adds as I flinch, "I wedged it up good and tight against the desk this time." My mouth opens and closes several times during this last statement, like a landed, gasping fish. I am as speechless as a fish would be on unexpected ground.

George unceremoniously waves at his pick-up outside the office window behind him. "*Then* I got in my Ford and came over here." He looks up at me from his perch. "So, is my leg broke?"

After a quick mental review of the full story of George's climb, and fall, and climb again, I am finally able to respond. I take a deep breath and tell him, "I appreciate you considered coming to me for assistance first, but I *do not* have x-ray vision to check for any broken bones." It is his turn to give me a withering look.

"Really, George, there is not much I can safely do except take you to the nearest urgent care to get an x-ray. Then I can be sure of what kind of injury we are dealing with."

However, true to his nature, George strongly resists any assistance in that respect, muttering on his way out the door that he got himself here, so what's another mile down the road? I hold the door to allow the dragging leg to clear fully, watching in wonder and helplessness as he pulls himself up into his pickup and drives off.

Luckily, George has sustained no breaks to his aged bones. He calls from home a few hours later, making an appointment to see me the next day. His injury is just a contusion, a large purple bruise over his left hip and side of his thigh, with the accompanying sore muscles.

So, after a few physical therapy sessions, George announces he is once more "fixed," shuffling his feet around in what he calls dance steps, but which I am sure would have been dangerous to the toes of any dance partner.

I shake his hand and wish him well.

Until next time.

CHAPTER 12

Three Potato …

On a personal note, I called my Dad on his eighty-first birthday. Both my parents were quite fit at that time, but living six hundred miles away in Western Oregon.

The phone rang and rang. As it continued ringing, much longer than usual, I was getting a bit worried. If my parents aren't literally sitting next to the phone in their kitchen, reading the paper, or watching the tiny TV that sits on the worn and faded counter top, they are making "social" shopping trips to the big warehouse stores. I call them "social" as my Mom is not so keen on visitors at home, but will carry on a very animated conversation with a total stranger, or the familiar cashier at Costco whom she knows by name. On these outings, my Dad usually forwards the home number to their cell phone.

So, calling on his birthday, I let the phone ring a few more times, then my mother, also in her eighties, finally picked up the receiver and gasped out, "Hello?" She was clearly out of breath and breathing hard. I thought, *Oh, no!*

"Hi Mom. Are you okay?" I blurted out. "Where were you, that you had to run for the phone?"

"Running" is not an exaggeration for the way my mother moves. It is something I can easily envision for this five-foot Mexican powerhouse, aka Rocky (her nickname from semi-pro softball in the Fifties), powering in from somewhere in the backyard. Most likely up a hill, to boot.

"I was just outside." She was still short of breath, but quickly recovering her voice. "I was holding the ladder for your papa. He's up on the roof," she clarified.

My heart leaped into my mouth.

"What?!" I loudly yelped. "What is he doing on the roof? And who is holding the ladder now?"

I imagined my father's stooped, white-haired form dangling from his fingertips on the gutter, his old and well worn work boots kicking frantically to find the ladder. The ladder that was now lying on the ground.

"Oh," my mother lazily replied. "Well, no one. Who else is around?" She laughed a little, but her tone of voice implied my question was silly. "He's fine," she started to say.

"Mom!" I interrupted, which is never a great thing to do with my mother. "Please! Go back out and hold the ladder!"

My thoughts flipped wildly from one scenario to another. What would have tempted my dad to climb up onto the roof in the first place? Ladders and roofs are just invitations to slip, stumble and fall, at least in my *professional* experience—not from climbing roofs, but for treating the resultant injuries from the falls that occur.

My thoughts raced, like my heart. *Why didn't he call a chimney sweep, or a roofer, or any other person who is paid to risk his neck on higher surfaces?*

This was my father! An eighty-one-year-old retired dentist, for Heaven's sake! I quit my mental ranting and returned to my phone conversation.

My mother had remained ominously silent and I knew she was upset with me for using "that tone of voice" and telling her what to do.

Now she was saying, "Ah! Here's your papa. He must be finished getting the moss off the roof." She quickly put down the phone before I could reply, letting it smack the kitchen table's hard surface, making a loud *crack*! in my ear. A not-too-subtle way of making me very aware she is irritated with me. I released a frustrated sigh, covering my eyes with my free hand and shaking my head in frustration. My dad moves at a more leisurely pace than his wife, so it took a couple minutes for him to pick up the phone. I heard him carefully clear his throat before talking.

"Hi, sweetheart!" My father's cheerful voice came over the line. He was obviously alive and well. I sighed and my heart, still pounding rapidly in my chest from concern and helplessness, started to slow a little. He added, "How are you?"

That gave me pause. *How am I?* Relieved, upset with my parents' apparent recklessness, frustrated at the distance between us,... and feeling guilty for not being there to help out my aging parents. Not a good mix of feelings that sat like a bag of restless snakes on my chest. I tried to shake it off before answering my dad.

"I called to wish you happy birthday, Pop!" Then I couldn't help myself and added, "But what the heck were you doing up on the roof, with only Mom to hold a ladder?"

Despite my attempts to sound calm, I heard the nagging edge to my voice. I dislike confronting my folks like this, but just what was he thinking?! Climbing up onto their steep, slippery roof... at his age?

Harry the Mule ... and Other Injuries

"That's no big deal." He chuckled a little. "I had a rope tied to me and I was watching my footing."

Now that I could hear his voice and knew my parents were safe, I finally took a step back mentally, starting to feel a bit ashamed at my outburst. I know my father is neither foolish nor impulsive in his decisions. For years in his youth, he'd climbed mountains and dived into caves. He is still generally quite fit, exercising daily. He was raised to fix things himself, and we, his children, always brought our broken toys, bikes, and even cars for him to repair. Not a day went by that my Father wasn't tinkering with a project or repairing some item my mom had brought home from a junk shop to save money.

Both my parents were products of the Depression. *Waste not, want not.* So, naturally, home repairs and roof maintenance were not out of their realm of do-it-yourself chores.

My mother loves to dig in the yard year-round and, as I mentioned earlier, played semi-pro softball in her youth. Not only that, but she sustained a household, chasing around her four children, then twelve grandchildren, and now four great-grandchildren. This couple is neither sedentary nor sedate.

I released a mental sigh this time, to clear my anxiety. Then I conversed with my father more casually, changing back to the subject of his birthday and other plans he might have besides climbing up on two-story buildings.

He is safe, I reassured myself. He had taken precautions, even if his only helper was my mother. And my mom was also right; who else was there, with the closest of their four children a full two hours away?

My parents' safety awareness and calmness have forced me to consider why people get so worried about their aging parents. Not only because *they* appear to be more fragile, feeble, or old. It makes *us* aware of our own mortality, thus becoming fearful of our own limitations as we age.

We become afraid to take chances, as the years go by. Those new experiences and adventures we may have exposed ourselves to in our younger years suddenly become evident in looking at our parents. It's like looking into our own future to see the changes occurring in our parents, such as arthritis, weakness from injuries, and loss of balance from sitting more and moving less.

It's like looking into a time machine, showing us how short our lives become on the other side of fifty—or at least, the potential to go in that direction.

Often the problems we see plaguing our parents have resulted from their giving into those myths of needing to slow down as you age. Our concern about the consequences of being active, such as sore muscles or joints, makes us change our approach to life. Instead of "Yes, I can!" the inner dialogue changes to "No, I cannot." Then we project this fear about our own aging onto our supposedly vulnerable parents. We tell our older, wiser parent, "Please don't stand on that!" from six hundred miles away, trying to govern their choices and limit their ability to enjoy themselves in continued independence. An independence none of us wants to give up.

CHAPTER 13

More ...

THE REALITY IS, NO matter what your age, you are faced with choices each and every day which will affect your safety and your longevity.

Such as driving in cars.

In the United States, we drive almost everywhere, even just down the block to a grocery store, although, we often don't think about the fact that our bodies are traveling thirty to seventy miles per hour. However, our bodies are designed for top speeds of fifteen miles per hour, in short sprints, which is why injuries that humans sustain in car accidents are akin to putting a mouse in a coffee can and shaking it (albeit the mouse most likely will not have airbags and a seat belt).

Putting aside the practical loss of the exercise achieved by a walk to the store, getting behind the wheel of a car offers risk of sustaining a serious or even life-threatening, injury. But the use of automobiles is an acceptable risk in our modern minds. Centuries ago, our ancestors found that riding a horse at top speeds of thirty-five m.p.h. got them where they had to go faster, and that too was an acceptable risk.

We have places to go and things to do! It is only human to want to get there faster.

So, as we age, how do we balance the desire for active living with less pain?

The trick is to not hold back because of fear, but to move forward with increased *awareness* and *wisdom*. The awareness to make choices that get us where we want to go and do the things we want to do … and the wisdom to know our limitations, lessening our risk of injury. It is a constant battle of choices and decisions. A proverbial juggling of how to have fun and stay alive.

So what did my dad teach me about awareness and wisdom on his eighty-first birthday? If you're going to dance on rooftops, be sure you have a rope and watch your footing.

Happy birthday, Pop.

CHAPTER 14

I Don't Want to Look Like That

MERLENE, A NEW CLIENT, walks into my clinic in a rush, her handbag the size of a football player's gym bag, forcing her to lean appreciably to the opposite side. Her face is tense and serious. Behind the furrowed brow and frown, Merlene is an attractive, blondish, thirty-something computer engineer who has come to me because she can no longer ignore the discomfort in her upper body The pain has built up for months, she writes on her evaluation paperwork, interfering with sleep, recreation, driving, even holding a utensil when eating. The attached body diagram on which I ask new clients to mark their pain is completely shaded in from the waist up, with bold handwriting next to it reading, "It all hurts!"

When I ask her to tell me what she thinks might be causing her pain, she states, "My mother has this huge hump on her back." She pauses, her anxiety visible. Then she asks me, "Is that going to happen to me, too? I don't want to look like that! But whatever else could be causing all this pain?"

Merlene looks at me with pleading eyes, afraid of my answer. However, hope hangs in her question, that maybe something other than an inherited spine problem can be to blame for the steady increase in her pain. As she indicated, months of pain preceded this visit, but the last straw was the inability to complete her work tasks. Merlene, like so many people, have this idea that they must "tough it out," not complain, keep their nose to the grindstone, and keep working until they drop at their desk—the vision of a truly dedicated employee.

Now this intense and normally very self-assured woman is sitting in a defeated pose, slumped back in her chair, and baffled how she came to be in my office. She is definitely rounding forward through the shoulders and upper back, but no more than many folks I have treated who also work all day on computers.

A side note: There has been an exponential progression in work-related injuries for office employees since the 1980s, when the cubicle era really took off, due to the mass production of "magical" computers that could create money for businesses at the speed of light. (Yes, that was typed with sarcasm.) Workers were placed at standard desks, in standard chairs, with their own desktop computers, also standard. The corporate dream was to have worker bees tied to a desk, working productively in one place for hours on end. Initially, I am sure that millions of dollars were generated in a short period of time ... at least, until the avalanche of pain issues began to bury corporations' money-making dreams in worker's-compensation lawsuits. Production-stopping ailments like carpal tunnel, migraines, tennis elbow, and sciatica were once limited to heavy lifting or car accidents. Now people were getting injured just sitting at a desk. How could that be?

Repetitive injury is the term used in the medical world to describe just what it says; an injury created by repeating a movement. These are muscle and tendon injuries. Overuse of these structures is similar to bending a paperclip back and forth, over and over. The movement creates friction, friction creates heat, and then, eventually, *snap!* Something breaks loose, or tears, or cramps up. Again, the body has made an executive decision to shut you down because it senses whatever you are doing is damaging.

So the big-business boom of cubicles and one-size-fits all computer desk set-ups caused companies to be overwhelmed with worker's-compensation claims and payment of medical costs, as the worker bees started to fail physically. Productivity dropped off and profit sank.

Because each person is unique in stature, flexibility and strength, it became clear that a unique workplace was needed for each worker bee. In other words, enough of this hive mentality. Laws were passed to protect a worker from getting injured on the job and to allow each individual the right to have an ergonomically correct desk set-up. Just another example of how the Rule of Pain will stop the wheels of progress. And just what is this Rule of Pain?

Pain instructs the human body, through various forms of discomfort, to pay attention to possible danger, like taking your hand off a hot stove. Without pain to trigger the reflex to snap your hand away quickly from destructive heat, you would soon be missing a few fingers. Not a pretty thought, I know, but our sense of pain actually keeps us alive each day.

Pain demands the body make changes in how we do things as a form of protection. One way this affects most desk workers is the repeated clicking of a computer mouse over and over, the supporting arm held at a weird angle because the desk is too high. Ultimately, if we insist on pushing through the rising muscle irritation in our forearm, the brain-body connection will make the rest of the body do contortions to get away from this pain. Consequently, I have seen some very "twisted" bodies in my time. Most of my clients are confused by this horrible onset of pain, like Merlene, the computer engineer still sitting in front of me. Merlene has informed me that she works ten-hour days, entering some fantastical coding into the most high-tech computer around. This includes two display monitors, an ergonomic keyboard, and a wireless mouse, all up on a deep, ginormous desktop, with the best office chair money can buy.

I shake my head silently, already knowing Merlene's pain is most likely related to how she is pushing her body through a ten-hour day, sitting in that fancy chair, surrounded by all that awesomeness of technology, yet not letting her muscles "breathe."

Yes, I said *breathe*. To function properly, oxygen must feed every cell of your body, bone to skin. Without proper circulation of oxygen and nutrients into muscles, they starve, and waste products build up with no escape. A working muscle is tight, bloodflow reduced, and it relies on moments of rest to bring in fresh blood supplies to stay healthy. When the muscles don't get the rest they require, then they begin to call for help.

So the initial message for help begins with a burning sensation. Then an ache slowly builds, creeping out to include a larger area. Next the pain signals really begin to talk. Maybe some sharp stabs or tingling sensations are added to the pot of symptoms. When this discomfort continues to be ignored, the body then pulls out all it final card and shuts you down. Numbness encases the limb, with muscles that refuse to follow your commands, and often cramp to the point of locking up and playing dead.

Sound familiar? Remember Sharon shaving her mule, Harry, back in chapter one? Most people have experienced a good old-fashioned charley horse in their leg after walking or standing longer than usual: intense cramping and pain, which cause you to do what? *Move*! You jump up from sitting, or roll out of bed, because the most common occasion for charley horse attacks to occur is when you have just drifted off to sleep. The sudden grab-and-stab of the cramping muscle makes you hop and dance. In other words, the pain is making you move the muscles, thus pumping life-giving oxygen and nutrients back into the cells. Move!

Simple, right?

Well, not when the highly developed, self-absorbed human brain is focused intently on a project deadline, ignoring all these early messages of cell starvation and overuse. Eventually the body wins the argument, possibly laughing as it chants, "Dance, you fool, dance!"

I return to my interview with Merlene, who is convinced her pain is caused by a genetic problem like a spine deformity. I ask her, "What do you mean by a 'huge hump'?" referencing her description of her mother's back.

"Well, she just keeps bending forward, more and more, over time," Merlene responds. "And my uncle is the same way. Kind of a hunchback, like that the one in the story."

I blink, puzzled for a moment. "You mean Quasimodo?"

"Exactly!" she responds. " Except Uncle George lives in Idaho Falls, not France, obviously." *Obviously*, I silently agree, covering my smile by keeping my head down as I write notes.

Merlene rushes on. "Uncle George would come to visit most summers. But he could never look you directly in the face because he was so bent over." Her voice is now a bit tremulous as I have still not answered her original question: *Is that going to happen to me, too?*

Having finished my examination of her spine and posture, I answer truthfully.

"No." I give her a reassuring smile. "The 'Quasimodo' syndrome does not need to affect you, or your children, if you do something about it now." Her eyes light up and she smiles back.

I go into the details of how genetics may bring increased chances of postural changes, but they do not necessarily *have to* occur. Education and awareness are the needed tools. *If,* I emphasize with a direct look in her eyes, she is willing to apply these tools.

Merlene assures me she will do anything to be rid of her pain and the fear of becoming a hunchback like Uncle George.

CHAPTER 15

Sharpening the Tools: Education and Awareness

I HAVE SOME SYMPATHY FOR Merlene's fear, as I remember my own worries over similar familial genetics and the strange twists of fate affecting a loved one's physical appearance. My own father, grandmother, and great-grandfather all exhibited a true degeneration of the upper spine into that "hunchback" posture.

My education taught me that this degeneration results from a form of rheumatoid arthritis called *ankylosing spondylitis*, where the joints attaching one vertebra to the next develop swelling and arthritic changes, eventually fusing the vertebrae together in one piece. The outcome is often a bent-forward posture due to the natural tendency to move away from the pain. The individual steadily leans further and further forward, creating the "Quasimodo" effect. My own family background includes this arthritic condition, and my father's occupation as a dentist exacerbated it by keeping him regularly in this bent position. In his eighties, his previously six-foot frame is uncomfortably, and permanently, bent to a mere five feet, five inches.

Growing up, I was terrified of this familial trend. I refused to allow my spine to be bowed forward, and was nicknamed "the princess" as I forced myself upright to the point of almost leaning backward through the majority of my teen years. I ended up giving myself joint problems anyway: mid-back cramping and irritation from forcing this posture for so long.

When I was in my early twenties and in physical-therapy school, the pain became too much to ignore. I spoke to my instructors about it, expressing similar concerns to Merlene's some twenty-five years later.

Consequently, I became an in-class example of over-posturing, a compensation opposite of the slouch mode. I learned there was a choice, either way. We can learn to find a balance and improve our body awareness, which I have strived toward all these years. My pain was resolved, replaced with firsthand knowledge that through willingness to make some changes, it is possible to be without pain. Ta-da! The lights went on and I have tried to share the revelation with anyone who will listen.

I have also seen the effects of genetics in the growth patterns of my children, especially my first son. At birth he was this bigger-than-life baby that the nurses dubbed "the little man" due to his muscular, nine-and-a-half pounds. He progressed off the charts in growth, looking like a three-month-old at only three weeks of age. We called him the Michelin Baby, like the tire mascot, due to the rolls of fat he added. He was a good eater from the start.

I'm sure he is loving me for sharing all this.

Anyway, when he was a year old, I began to worry. *Will he never get legs?* I was very proud that my big, healthy baby was always way above the norms for size, with a head larger than mine and a stout upper body. However, his lower body had short, bowed legs. His clothing was composed of size-four toddler tops that I had to stretch the neck of to pull over his head, paired with twelve-month-old pants. The disproportion was scary. Was he going to be a dwarf?

My pediatrician was unperturbed. Sure enough, by his second birthday, he sprouted long legs to match his upper body. He continued to exceed the growth charts, so when he was only five years old, he was too tall to stick in the bathtub, making it difficult to really get all the dirt off. And as anyone who has raised an active five-year-old boy knows, it was *imperative* to get one layer of dirt off before adding another the next day.

So I decided to introduce him to taking showers. There he was, getting his first lesson in taking a shower, with me giving direction from behind the curtain, trying to keep a discreet eye on him as he stood on a slippery tub surface. He did fine, scrubbing the layers of grime off his feet and knees. He remained steady under the shower's spray, and all was going well, until I had him tip his head back under the stream to wet his hair for shampooing.

A most unexpected thing happened. He started to fall backward. *Timber!* Just like a tree, there was not even a hint of bend to his spine. His toes came up as he rocked onto his heels.

I quickly darted my hand in and caught his upper back to keep him from smacking his head against the shower wall. He was a bit startled, as was I, but I was able to get him to attempt tipping his head back again.

Instant replay. Even with my "professional" direction, my son couldn't even begin to arch his lower back to compensate as his head tipped into the shower spray.

Okay. Time to think.

Harry the Mule ... and Other Injuries

Sharpening the Tools: Education And Awareness

This movement—what I considered a *normal* action, i.e., a person tipping his head back to wet his hair under a shower, or even just to look up—seemed impossible for him. I was worried, but still had a wet, dirty-haired child to deal with, so I just had him turn around to face the shower and wash his hair.

Just like his father does.

Hmmm...Just like his father.

The proverbial lightbulb flashed in my brain. Maybe this was genetic?

What if it was just not *natural*, or part of the inherited "wiring," that made it difficult for my husband and son to arch their backs in the shower? Did my son's father, and *his* father before him, use trial and error to come up with an option? Like simply turning around to do the same task?

My son could easily perform a backward arch while laying on his stomach, and even when standing on the living room floor. Just not in the shower. I have to admit, I never saw his dad fall down in a parking lot while looking up at a plane in the sky, so who knows why a shower is different? I had no answer.

This simply was how they were from birth.

So what is "normal"? What is "natural"? And, what should I really expect of my family and clients?

Because I have a son who made me question what should be considered "normal," I never again expected everyone to move in the same manner to do the same tasks. In other words, "There is more than one way to skin a cat." Or, to wash your hair, as in this case.

And, no, I have never asked my eldest son, now thirty-three years old and six foot four, "Do you still face the shower to wash your hair, or do you tip your head back?"

I don't care, as long as his hair gets washed.

CHAPTER 16
Meet The Parents

"Chalk ... Chalk!" my mother yells at my dad from the kitchen. He is clear across the house, but makes his way quickly at that familiar beckon of his wife of over fifty years.

For most of my young life, I thought my dad's name was "Chalk." My mother was raised in Arizona, of Mexican descent, and placed a unique accent on words which turned my father from "Chuck," short for Charles, to "Chalk."

I had many a friend ask me, "Did your mom just call your dad 'Chalk'?"

"Chalk" and Rowena built an interesting foundation for my life, leading up to my becoming a physical therapist.

My father is known as the "pain-free dentist," no small feat to attain. He could give an injection without creating fear and pain. He would chat amiably as he maneuvered sharp instruments in a patient's mouth, his hand steady, his voice gentle and soothing. He often would treat low-income and mentally disabled clients that no one else wanted to take on.

Partly, the other dentists deferred their services due to poor return on their billing, but mostly, many of these folks needed the patience and caring attitude that my father shared with everyone entering his clinic.

At times, payment was accomplished through the barter system with those who had no cash and no insurance. They often did have a talent, or vocation, to trade with my Dad for services. The house was re roofed, works of art produced, but mostly, it was the "thank you for helping me" that my father accepted in payment.

My mother, was a constant example of helping others. She helped care for disabled children in the public schools, volunteered at hospitals and made home visits for a hospice organization, spending time and finding ways to help people too ill to leave their homes.

She also kept a steady pot of food on the stove for us four always-hungry children and our friends. In her spare time, she took on creative antique refinishing or decorative projects that she might, or might not, finish. It didn't really matter. She was happiest when taking something apart, just to see if she could put it back together in better condition and functional.

My mother was also a Spanish interpreter for the city and was called upon for various duties to assist in communication. At one point, she recognized that another population needed interpretation in certain situations: the hearing impaired. So she took night classes to learn sign language. We practiced with her, learning some basic signs and the alphabet. What a gift I have found this to be in my own interactions with clients I now treat.

Even if I'm not treating a Spanish-speaking or hearing-impaired individual, the exposure to my young mind that communication is not an impossible barrier makes me brave enough to take on all languages and situations.

"Will you treat this woman? She is new to this country and needs physical therapy but has been badly abused in her past." The voice on the phone has the unmistakable sound of pleading. I occasionally get these calls from social workers, psychologists, and state caseworkers, all asking for help for an individual of similar circumstances.

Often by the time the call is made to my office, the individual has already been turned down by other facilities, clinics and practitioners. Sometimes this reluctance is due to the language barrier, but often it stems from the practitioner's unwillingness to confront the emotional "wall" around these clients: a protective wall that is incredibly difficult to breach, caused by their fear of being touched by anyone.

Abuse has built this wall, and it is neither rare nor limited to those new to our country. All I can see is a human being in pain and in need of my skills, not only physically, but emotionally and mentally as well. They look as if their souls are bruised, and my heart goes out to them all.

"How can I best help them?" I always ask myself, questioning my ability to really make a difference. My hesitation lasts a millisecond. Then I dive in with all my heart.

Of course, I provide hours of entertainment to my initially apprehensive clients, recent immigrants from Vietnam, Uganda, Bosnia, Yugoslavia, various South American countries, and provinces of Mexico.

Suddenly they are faced with this tall, energetic, and animated woman who is gesticulating wildly, mimicking pain, holding an arm, dragging a limb, or stooping over with mimed back pain. My attempts at their native language (I always learn how to say "pain" in their language), are often met with a chorus of giggles and head-shaking. While I fill in the blanks with my extravagant body language, my behavior conveys that I am of no threat, and usually provokes outright laughter.

Mission accomplished. Down comes the wall. Let the healing begin.

So what did I really learn from my parents?

To not be afraid. To try, and accept that I may fail. Possibilities of failure follow each of us every day, every time we climb out of bed.

The list of things to do is never ending, with the idea of failure at times blocking us from even trying. Yet potential failure is never the right reason to avoid making an attempt at something, especially if it benefits another person. Because if you try and succeed in the trying, you may accomplish something worthy and memorable.

This behavior was, and still is, my parents' goal. I am proud to say that I still carry that torch and hope to see my own children continue such a wonderful tradition.

Harry the Mule ... and Other Injuries

CHAPTER 17

Parental Guidance Recommended

Sometimes we add things—electronic things—to our lives that involve danger.

Our initial intention to have these things is good: a weed trimmer to keep the yard looking good; a toaster to prepare that breakfast bagel more quickly; or a treadmill to exercise with—part of being healthy and well, right?

It is all good until a rock flies into your leg via the weed trimmer, or the toaster catches the bread on fire and you try to fish it out with a metal fork (please don't), or, in the case of my parents, the new treadmill that has so much technology, it literally sweeps you off your feet.

My father told me this story during one of our weekly check-in phone conversations.

Now approaching eighty-four years old, my father informed me that the dinosaur-like treadmill they had used for nigh on twenty years finally had to be replaced—something about my mother not wanting to deal with the unraveling tread snagging and jerking her to full halts while in use.

The new treadmill arrived in several pieces, which was good, since it was to be placed in their basement. Carrying it downstairs involved navigating steep steps that took two right turns. I purposely neglected to ask how the old treadmill made it out, but that will be another story, I'm sure.

Piece by piece the new treadmill made it down the stairs and was assembled by my father. It was a new and very high-tech machine. My father was itching to get on this thing. He stepped on the back of the treadmill, reached forward toward the glowing digital panel of lights to get the machine started, and pushed the *wrong* button.

Instead of a smooth, gentle walking speed, he was suddenly launched—literally—into a fast-paced jog. His feet flew to keep up with the wild machine, but, he noted, his legs rapidly moved farther behind his upper body, which was still anchored by both hands to the safety grips at the front of the machine.

He desperately tried to pull the emergency shut-off cord, his snow-white hair and glasses bouncing in time to the rapid pace and odd body angle. However, by the time he was able to release one of his hands, he had traveled too far back on the machine's tread and the bright red cord remained out of his reach.

Finally, he lost his footing altogether, striking a knee on the fast-moving tread as he went down. My father described "bouncing" off the treadmill into a humiliated heap on the carpeted floor.

Do recall that I was six hundred miles away as he related this story to me, his daughter, a health professional. I should have been concerned and expressing worry, yet I could not stop laughing. The mental image of my eighty-four-year old father hustling along on a possessed treadmill, like a scene out of a cartoon, was all too much! I could almost hear the Looney-Toons theme and Porky Pig stuttering out, "Thadabe, thadabe…that's all folks!"

Obviously, he had survived to tell the tale, my mother adding elaboration in the background about all the noise his crash-landing made, so the levity of the situation was allowed. Even though I repeatedly apologized for my response—once I could stop laughing, that is—my father was also chuckling. He then wondered out loud, "Why in the world would an emergency cord be at the front of a machine, when it is off the back you will be falling?"

Good question.

CHAPTER 18

"Go for The Burn!" Then See Your Physical Therapist

Okay, so we've covered a large number of scenarios that many of us have been through. Mishaps. Some of our own choice, and some that come out of the blue. However, one area we most certainly have a choice about is our chosen form of exercise.

Most Americans believe they must exhaust themselves on a daily basis, either in their jobs, their extracurricular activities, or both. We present ourselves as a society of masochists, hell-bent on inflicting as much pain in a day as possible, and thinking to ourselves, as we collapse into a pile of mush, "It must have been a good day. I hurt everywhere!" Rarely is this statement accompanied by a true sense of accomplishment, or more importantly, a smile.

Yes, smiling is very important to that part of your internal chemistry that creates healing. If you aren't healing, after all the torture you put yourself through, then tomorrow is *not* going to be a better day!

Despite the TV ads and "reality" shows that depict people exercising like Olympians, our bodies really, really, REALLY need periods of rest to work best. Somewhere between the couch-potato and the two-hour workout to look like Zeus is where your body purrs along like a well-oiled machine.

Maintenance, not over use.

Moderate challenges, not abuse.

And rest. Rest of the mind as well as the body provide balance to your internal chemistry. This balance is needed to promote healing and repair. *This* is what keeps you young.

Push too hard and you actually age faster!

What? you may be asking. Isn't exercise supposed to hurt? Once again, the answer is NO!

Pain is a warning of damage, right? No one (of sound mind) really believes that hitting their hand repeatedly with a hammer is healthy. Repeated injury breaks down and destroys muscle fiber, eventually forming scar tissue. Healthy muscle tissue is elastic and absorbs shock. Fibrotic, scarred tissue is a tangled mess of tough, resistant fibers, like those hopelessly snarled knots in your string of Christmas lights. Not exactly spring-loaded material to help you bounce out of bed in the morning.

Just get a new set, right? Christmas lights, maybe, but not muscles and joints. You just can't go down to the superstore and pick up a new set of those. This is more complicated and less accurate for what you get in return for your efforts.

Actually, the formula is quite simple.

If you train with pain, you will create more pain fibers and less healthy muscle. If you train without pain and allow the body to feel safe, then hey! Guess what? There's no need for those extra pain fibers! Amazing!

Rumi was a wise philosopher and observer of man who lived over six hundred years ago. He said, *"These pains you feel are messengers. Listen to them."*

Six hundred years later, I beseech you to heed this advice. Listen to your body's messages. It is wise and wants to help you.

CHAPTER 19

Enough Said

WITHIN THE STORIES AND narrations included in this little book, there are ideas and thoughts related to how to avoid pain and injury and sustain wellness, i.e., balance, to get thorough life.

We all do the best we can, each day, in our own way. Smile and laugh each day, for your benefit, as well as for those around you.

I extend to you, best wishes in health.